HOW TO LOVE A WOMAN

HOW TO LOVE A WOMAN

Gregory O. Chiadika, PhD, Fth

CONTENTS

INTRODUCTION

Have you ever been asked for your advice about a woman, wife or sister? Where do you begin, how do you start to explain to the person the complexity of the feminine gender? How do you in one-hour counseling session cover all the uniqueness of one of God's most priceless creation? The dynamics of her entire makeup, fragile yet extremely strong, gentle yet very forceful, easily misunderstood yet very clear to see, transparent and at the same time a well of secrets. Having the ability to create and destroy at the same time. You really cannot tell of her unless you really know her.

At her creation, man was put in a deep sleep, near death. God needed her to be in the scene of life singularly represented. Man at first sight recognized her amongst other creations and gave her that befitting name – Woman.

Through the years and decades after creation she became different image to different people, most misunderstood and very much unloved and cared for. Those who claim to lover her, do that doe what they stand to gain from her. So through, the years of my counseling, many would ask me the question "How do I love this woman?", sometimes you come across those that have mastered the act of manipulation and seduction, and get away with hurting the woman they claimed to love – making it more difficult for the next man that comes her way.

In this book, I will attempt to unravel the mystery behind loving a woman, and be able to help those who are in the valley of frustration in their relationship with their woman. Also procuring solutions and positive guidance to developing a better relationship with the woman in your life. Read with care and pay attention to your heart as God will definitely whisper to you.

Remember, knowledge is not knowledge until the truth acquired is put into practice.

CHAPTER ONE

WHO IS A WOMAN?

Woman has different meaning to different people. She is often defined by the personal experience the person has had with the women in his life.

Generally, a woman is the feminine Gender, one referred to as the Adult Female. From theological view point a woman is the man with the wombs, one taken from the side of the man, the man's front.

In the home, she is the wife to a husband, the mother to children, the home keeper, solution bringer, someone who nurtures, natural lover, an epitome of strength. She is the core of life to the family and society at large. She is a reservoir where you draw from and a bank where you deposit all your worries and hurts. Dutiful manager of the home, husband and children.

Her nature carries with it certain helpful qualities; she is naturally a detailed person and observer with vivid mind making her able to easily detect problems before they surface and also able to procure solutions to the problems on ground. She thinks deep and looks beyond the surface. Above all she is easily faithful, cleaves to relationship, finds it difficult to forget people and the help they have rendered to her, she does not forget. She is very emotional and easily understanding.

All these qualities make up an average woman; these qualities however can become a disadvantage if applied in the negative. People who know these qualities take advantage of the woman and unfortunately make the worse of them. The same water we drink, when heated up can burn the person up. A woman is frail, easily broken, and weak. The bible says the same.

"Likewise, ye husbands, dwell with them according to knowledge, giving honor unto the wife, as unto the weaker vessel and as being heirs together of the grace of life; that

your prayers be not hindered" 1 Peter 3:7 (NKJV)

Here we see God protecting the woman and telling us that the way we treat the woman in our life can stop Him (God) from answering our prayers.

MAN WITH THE WOMB

A woman is naturally endowed with the qualities of incubating the seed that is implanted into her. She is a multiplier of fertilized eggs. Whatever is put in her, she multiplies. God looked down at the man he had made and saw that he needed to separate the womb from the man and he made a woman. Seeds fertilized in her are naturally multiplied. The seed doesn't only multiply in her but it is also kept alive and growing in her till it is given birth to. Your wife is what you make her!!!

Make a woman and you are making a people, nation, world with a woman by your side, you will be multiplied. You will not remain alone for too long. Only remember, it's the seed you plant that she multiplies – either good or bad!!! You may remain alone for a few until you recognize the woman or women God has given to you to multiply your vision. You need them.

"The Lord gave the word: great was the company (of women) of those that published it" Psalm 68:11. The company of those in the original text connotes Feminine gender.

Just as you can't multiply good without women so also you cannot multiply evil without women. Women are instruments of change; Rosa Louise McCauley Parks was an American activist in the civil rights movement best known for her pivotal role in the Montgomery bus boycott. The United State Congress has called her "The first lady of civil rights" and "the mother of the freedom movement"

The world's longest serving monarch is Queen Elizabeth II: 1926 – Present day – 66 years running.

Clara Barton, civil war nurse and founder of the American Red Cross. Dorothy Levitt, pioneers of automotive racing. Helen Keller, author, activist, and the first deaf and blind person to earn a Bachelor of Arts degree. Mary Mitchell Slessor Scottish Presbyterian Missionary to Nigeria, stopped the killing of twins in Calabar. She adopted all the abandoned babies, founded and cared for them at the mission house.

Aimee Semple Mcpherson was a Canadian-American Pentecostal evangelist and media celebrity in the 1920s and 1930s, famous for founding the foursquare church.

Time will not permit us to talk about other women like Kathryn Kullman, who pioneered the teachings of the Holy Spirit, Harriet Tubman an American abolitionist and political activist born into slavery, who escaped and subsequently made some 13 missions to rescue approximately 70 enslaved people, including family and friends, using the network of antislavery activists and safe houses known as the Underground Railroad. Women who were fearless and relentless in their pursuit to better the lives of others and mankind in general. Women are world changers. The known Smith Wigglesworth's wife dress up in black, was confronted by her husband why and she said "God was dead" Wigglesworth laughed and said "God can't die" she replied him saying "If God is not dead, why are you not preaching".

Wigglesworth rose up, carried his bible and started preaching again never allowing depression to set in again. Women are weak but a mighty tool in the hand of the Almighty God. After resurrection, Jesus Christ appeared first to a woman, she did not doubt but went and delivered the message to the others. Women are faithful to the end. Surrounded at the feet of the cross by women, who won't let go and were willing to die for what or who they believe.

CHAPTER TWO

UNDERSTANDING HER

The word understand means;

1. To grasp a concept fully and thoroughly, to be aware of the meaning of an (of people) to be aware of the intent of

2. To believe or impute

3. To stand underneath, to support

The scripture clearly states that true understanding is given by God

"But there is a spirit in man: and the inspiration of the Almighty giveth the understanding" Job 32:8, while verse 9 says

"Great men are not always wise: neither do the aged understand judgement".

This gives us the insight that understanding is not necessarily gotten by age or greatness but by inspiration from God.

Understanding a woman takes a conscious effort from the man who embarks in this journey. You just can't get it without seeking for it. this is where many people miss it, that you know things or that you are wise and maybe rich does not mean you understand women, that you understand women does not mean you will understand that woman – your wife, partner. Understanding is something you have to get.

"Happy is the man that findeth wisdom, and the man that getteth understanding" Proverbs 3:13

Some people may claim that certain woman is difficult and hard to get but a man who is able to understand her enjoys the privileges that comes with it.

"God understanding giveth favor: but the way of transgressors is hard" Proverbs 13:15

So the journey of understanding a woman begins with knowing what a woman is not.

- **Sex Object**

When a young girl begins to develop into a woman, she notices the special attention given to her by the opposite sex and the way he stares at her, especially at her breast and enlarged hips or backside. Naively she wonders why, some even ignorantly ask "why are you looking at me" or "why are you looking at me and not smiling". When she discovers that it's because the man would want to have sex with her, she feels disappointed at the person and sees the man as a dirty man, who just wants to disvirgin her, harm her, impregnate her or even transfer one disease or the other to her. So she runs from such person. Until she is told that it's not so bad after all, then the desire begins to grow in her for the opposite sex.

That feeling of not being seen as a sex object grows in every woman, she may want to have sex but she would not in any way want her partner to see her as a sex object; one whose only value is gotten in sex, one who is only good for sex – she hates it. every woman wants to be seen for who they are, their worth and value should be apart from giving sexual satisfaction to the man they are with.

She doesn't want to be of value to you only when you want but she wants you to respect her body and respect her feelings all the time – see her as fragile and beautiful, precious and a treasure not a cupboard for your needs or a dumping ground for your sperm. She would prefer that when you touch her, it is with ultimate care and tenderness, preferably with her complete permission. She wants you to know and acknowledge that it's her body and not yours to begin with.

The woman's body is built in a way that too much sex can cause harm than good, let the body relax and after a good time of making love, she would want to live with the memory of it for a while before you come again.

Most active men want sex daily or even more than once a day, but as a married man, you have to be careful so that it will not make your wife withdraw from you instead of cleaving to you. Her body is not only for sex, don't abuse it, it is the temple of God, holy and deserving of honor.

So if you are such a man that is guilty, you will have to really apologize to your wife and work on being a real man – a real man considers his wife's well-being.

- **Perfect**

Just because a woman is beautiful, sweet and at the same time lovely does not make her in anyway flawless – she has flaws – she's human. Her two legs and hands are not completely the same, and if you look more closely her two breast are not exactly the same size, they are different. No two identical twins are exactly the same. You just have to look closely.

The same goes with women. God never created two people the same nor did he place a stamp of flawlessness on any woman.

Every woman comes with her won complexity and uniqueness, and imperfection. Stop expecting too much from a woman. The one you have outside has her own faults in character, behavior, temperament and make-up.

Over-expectation can kill your relationship, take it or leave it, your wife is only human, see the flaws and leave with it, not in condemning her but in encouraging her to change or just simply live with it. Changing is one thing that only God can do, not man, if she is lazy with house chores, stop complaining, do what you can or pay someone to do it, if she cannot cook and is willing to learn, good for you, teach her or get someone to teach her. But if she is not just interested, then get a cook – find solutions that work for the two of you and move on. I hear some fast food sell prepared soup and dishes now. If she talks too much, you may have to receive grace to listen, at least get entertained by her. Be the balancing personality that she needs beside her and everything will work out fine. Remember that you snore 'phat loud' shout too much etc. and she lives with it, why can't you live with hers? You must develop a large heart to stay in a relationship for a long period of time, so also in marriage. Getting married does not change who we are, it in fact blows it up angels are perfect maybe that is why they are not married. There are no marriages in heaven. Everybody is perfect there. So marriages are for imperfect people – so therefore, celebrate your imperfections and just help each other work at it. If you have need of an expert, you can get one or go look for one that will help you or your spouse.

- **Gullible/ or stupid**

Consciously or unconsciously, men have the tendency to think that women are gullible or stupid. Emotionally maybe some women but being stupid and gullible is one thing an average woman is not.

One cannot deny the fact that emotional feelings have its play on all of us especially females; often blinded by the love and feelings they have for that person, denying their natural instincts and reasoning ability may fall a victim to a trickster or con man. When a woman loves, she loves deep and totally even though her eyes are wild open and she sees things clearly. She may decide to just follow and stay on the side of the one she loves. Women are good followers and naturally faithfully friends/lovers. You can always count on them. They don't easily forget the kindness done to them, neither do they forget to repay the evil done to them unless God stops them. If a woman is stupid, she chose to at her own volition not that she doesn't know better.

Abigail knew that her husband was a wicked and unreasonable man but she chose to stay with him, maybe because he was rich or there again just because he was her husband. She tried to appease David, saving her husband from immediate hurt and then securing her own future. Women always play to win. **1 Samuel 25:14, 18, 23, 32, 29, 42.** If you are having an affair, your wife might not know who but she will most likely know that something has changed about you and depending on how sensitive she is, she will definitely know that you are having an affair. From a distance, a woman can tell when a man is interested in her. She might want to follow through not because she wants an affair but because she enjoys the attention, gift and love you are giving to her. That is why it is always difficult for a woman to forgive when her love is betrayed, the heart of a woman has space for only one lover at a time unless in some unusual situations where the person is either distorted mentally or emotionally sick. Sometimes demonically infested or possessed. The most common today is demonic infestation via a sinful lifestyle and environment, TV shows, demonic films. Sometimes meeting some people who are highly demonically infested and fraternizing with them in an intimate manner. Some abusive past can make a woman to become withdrawn, gullible or become overprotective of her spouse. When she had been raped brutally or repeatedly, she would need healing to become normal again. We will talk more on these in the next chapter of the book.

- ### **Mechanical**

You can't be more further from the truth to think that a woman us mechanical or stereotyped in nature. No body embraces change like a woman; in marriage it's her surname that is changed and she embrace it gladly. She moves into her husband's house and world without complain. A woman us naturally flexible and adaptable to change, so long as the change is that which she desires and glad to have.

Complain only arises when it's not what was expected or desired. She would there again cry out for change to another new thing of the previous. No woman loves to suffer!

In the first place she was created after the man was in existence, there was an existing garden and man to tend to it. she came into the scene only as a solution to the obvious problems of man's companionship issue. One of her qualifications was that she was adaptable and complementary to the man.

So if your wife behaves in a manner you don't like mechanically or almost immediately, you may need to find out why and try to address the situation because she is not wired that way. If for instance she prepares rice and stews every afternoon, rather than attacking her for that, you may have to see if she has other options readily available ad also find out if the available options are the ones she is familiar with and can cook.

Generally speaking, women are not mechanical, they flow, adjust and blend easily. There are however situations where they are rigid and very mechanical, all you may need to so is to find out why, either from her, her parents or from God (the manufacturer). I used to think that my wife enjoyed wearing herself out with house chores until I got a house help who was very hardworking. Every woman enjoys rest and comfort believe me.

CHAPTER THREE

LOVING HER

Loving a woman may mean different things to different people. You may think you love your spouse but what you actually love is the thing between her legs. So truly loving a woman/ your wife require you to firstly;

DISCOVER HER UNIQUENESS

In counseling couple/ observe when you ask the man to tell you why he loves his wife and her uniqueness, they often end up telling you the physical attraction or the things they find attractive about her, and rarely mention her uniqueness.

Her uniqueness is that which distinguishes her from any other woman, her selling point. Her uniqueness which includes both her weakness and strength, that which makes her — her. That which no one can take away from her. Identical twins can look alike but if you really know them, you would discover that they are two different people – unique in every respect.

In discovering her uniqueness, you would have to spend quality time with her, stay around her; laugh with her, cry with her, play with her, walk with her, work with her, cook with her, go to places with her, eat together, bath together, watch movies together, go to church together, listen to her talk, I mean actually listen with your ear and heart, hear her tell you her story, listen to her complains, know her fears, her drive, get to know that which make her do the things she does – discover her. It is a process and the only thing you need is time and patience with an understanding heart.

KNOW HER NEEDS

Here is where many young couple fail and sometimes even older couple. In many cases she may not even know what she needs. you would have to find that out by yourself with the help of God.

Generally speaking, a woman needs;

1. Frequent demonstration of love and affection, because of her need for affection, daily expressions of romantic love are vital to a woman's existence. These are the basic key to her self-worth, satisfaction with married life and her sexual responsiveness. By consistently and thoughtfully expressing affectionate attention, many men could melt the heart of even the most frigid wife. "A woman's need for romantic attention and affection might be compared to an empty 55-gallon barrel. A smart man begins filling her barrel first thing in the morning. Before getting out of bed, he'll wrap his arms around her and whisper sweet nothings (five gallons). During breakfast he compliments her on something (another five). Before hustling out the door he gives her a hug and kiss (five more). During a coffee break he phones to let her know he is thinking of her (another five). At night when

he comes in the door, before greeting the kids or petting the dog he gives her a warm hug, a genuine smile and a kiss with some meaning (10 gallons). He compliments her on the evening meal (another five). Even through the chauffeurs the kids to and from a meeting, pays bills, and works on the computer, he gives her to minutes of his undivided attention to talk about something important (15 gallons), and he caresses her lovingly as they pass in the hallway (five). When he crawls into bed that night, he can be rest assured that he has filled her emotional love barrel to the 55-gallon mark (without spending a dime!)

As a man, you must make a conscious decision to express love.

2. Her need for emotional security.

Every woman looks for reassurance of a place in her husband's affections by asking him to do what she could easily do for herself, it's even better when he does things. She would have done without her telling him, his willingness serves as a measure of his love and adoration. Gives her a sense of emotional security.

While in the bedroom she might withdraw from her husband's sexual advances simply because she wants him to persist in his efforts despite all obstacles she puts in his way. If he doesn't, she concludes that he doesn't care anymore.

The man must let her know that she is the one for him and that he would choose her again and again.

3. Her Need for Appreciation for Domestic Efforts:

A woman wants to know that you care about her world. Regular sincere appreciation of the things she does tells her a load of things. Don't think that she knows, tell her! She wants to hear it from your mouth and see it in your eyes while you are saying it that you truly appreciate all that she does. Appreciation for her efforts to look attractive.

A woman needs to feel attractive. She needs to hear again and again that her husband finds her attractive. Make complimentary remarks on her looks, specifically and make sure you notice any new thing she dos to look different, when she makes a new style, buys new underwear, dress, make up etc. let her catch your eyes gazing at her, then smile and tell her she is amazing.

4. Romantic Attention

Romantic attention is not only when you want sex and move in to touching her and kissing her. Romantic attention is that hug you give her before parting for office, it's that smoothing of her hair in the public, that kiss in the church or at your office if she is around. Romantic attention is that extra effort you make in buying the things she loves so much that she never asked for. Romantic attention is that surprise gift on an ordinary day. Romantic attention is understanding your wife's love language and communicating it effectively; it could well be telling her to seat back while you cook, do the shopping because you know it will be more convenient for you to do, playing her favorite music and invite her to cuddle with you on the sofa while you listen, surprise pick after work, washing her back while she's in the tubor shower, hugging her for no reason, compliment her in front of a friend, changing her underwear's as a surprise. Women love pleasant surprises, well everybody does, but it does something to a woman that she cannot explain – releases romantic ecstasy all over the body. Whenever you go out of your way to do something to your wife without her asking, it only gives her an assurance that you love her.

Romantic attention is that gentle touch on her back side, that rubbing of her laps in the pubic while driving, that smile from afar, that squeezing of her hands in the public, that holding of each other without saying a word. No matter how rigid or hard a woman appears, she needs romantic attention.

Loving her entails knowing the fact that no feminine gender is uniquely different from the male. Hence special cognizance must be taken. Have a smooth loving relationship with her. Just like everybody else, she wants to be celebrated and cared for, not the way you want but the way that suits her gender and uniqueness as a person.

5. A woman needs to talk to feel close; she needs to talk especially about their feelings and problems. When she talks, she is simply exploring her feelings and when you stop it, she feels alienated from her mate. A woman talks in a search for intimacy, to gain her partners empathy and understanding as she would with her women friends, so just listen without interrupting and without offering advice. Talking makes her feel better, this is normal female behavior. She is expressing her

care and concern. What she is really doing is thinking out loud.

When your wife feels free to talk to you about anything, she will feel an intimacy and closeness that goes beyond her wildest dreams, then you can say you have both a lover, dearest friend and companion.

6. Honesty, openness and Trust,

Sometimes you need women who don't mind that you lie, but they would actually love it if you would lie to everyone else makes her to trust you and creates the atmosphere for her to be free with you, but when you are not open and very secretive, you give her mind up to wonder, and believe me an average woman's mind can wonder wild.

7. Commitment to family:

Remember that the woman did not exist without the man, but the man did, she was taken out of the man. That is why the man can work all day but for the woman the first thing she responds to is family, she came to man and man called her woman – man with the womb, for man; Genesis chapter one.

A woman needs her husband to understand how much she needs him to commit time and attention to the family unit. Demonstrate to the children that it is fun to be together as a family. Show them how cooperation, sharing, respect and encouragement are achieved. You must be willing to find time out of no time to achieve that, don't lie to yourself, it won't help your relationship with your wife or your children if you don't spend quality time with them.

CHAPTER FOUR

OBSTACLES TO LOVING HER

In loving a woman, a man faces certain obstacles, in this book we shall attempt to expose you some of them, knowing clearly that there are certain obstacles that are peculiar to an individual. I will try to highlight most of these obstacles;

HER PAST EXPERIENCE

A woman's personal experiences have a way to form who she is at home and with her husband. These experiences can go far back as her childhood days. If she was raised by loving and caring parents, she may have little or no problem responding to love and in fact showing love. She knows how to love; she also can receive love. But in a situation where she was raised in a hostile and uncaring environment; it becomes difficult for her to love and be loved. She simply does not know how; her belief system is that there is no true love and people are not to deserving of love

So, she is rash, irrational and very heartless in her dealings with people. And if the hurt is specifically incurred from a man, male figure, then her resentment towards men can be obvious and very deep. It becomes difficult to trust the opposite sex (men) again. Some of such women may end up becoming lesbians or bisexual. You will hear statement like "All men are alike", "Men are not worth it", "Life is easier without men" etc. from such people sometimes.

TOLERANCE LEVEL

People have different to tolerant level, whether male or female it's this tolerant level that can pass as an obstacle when it comes to loving her. Naturally speaking some people are short tempered and cannot tolerate certain persons or certain behavioral display. Most of such person also find it difficult to hide their feelings, once they cannot take it, they just turn off and the person cannot reach them anymore.

It's difficult but it is equally possible. You would have to discover how to effectively communicate with such person. At times, they might require you to hear them out, wait patiently before you react, find a way to see things from their point of view or better still try to understand why they are proving difficult, they might just need more persuasion from you. Not forcefully as some spouses try to but lovingly and patiently. It may require you to walk away from the scene at that given time and then come back later when they are calmer. They may be wrong but if they cannot see it, there is nothing you can do- "Relationship strife not because the guilty is punished but because the innocent is merciful".

You cannot quench fire with fire, find out why she is also short tempered; Stressed?

- Is she stressed?

- Is she sick, physically or mentally or even emotionally?

- Is she depressed?

- Does she have a low self-esteem and is fighting back?

- Could it be pride?

- Is she under any pressure, at work etc.?

- Is she dissatisfied about you?

- Is she dissatisfied about life generally?

- Does she have a piled up sad events or works?

- Is she angry with herself?

- Is she living in secret sin?

Once theses things can be handled am sure the issue with fade away unless of course it is a result of influence; external influences from a person, people or demons and demonic holds.

Where there are people involved you may have to disconnect her from such people to get her to see things differently. You may have to change neighborhood but where they are evil strong hold changing environment may not help.

You will have to deal with the strong hold, take authority bind the forces of darkness on her behalf and cast them far from her, you are her husband, you have some level of spiritual authority over her, use it in the place of prayer. They may be strong holds as old as three generations or more. Thank God for the authority we as believers in Christ have over the kingdom of darkness. *"Who hath delivered us from the power of darkness and hath translated us into the kingdom of his dear son"*. Colossians 1:13

"And I will give unto thee the keys of the kingdom of heaven; and whatsoever thou shalt bind on earth shall be bound in heaven: and whatsoever thou shalt loose on earth shall be loosed in heaven". Matthew 16:19.

"And he said unto them, I beheld Satan as lighting fall from heaven" Behold I give unto you power to trend on serpents and scorpions and over all the power of the enemy and

nothing shall by any means hurt you". Luke 10:18-19.

FALSEHOOD AND INSINCERITY FROM SPOUSE;

Falsehood is common with spouses that are insecure. They want to live a lie and sometimes it was how they got their wife, falsehood might help you get marry a woman but it will certainly not help you keep her. The very nature of women hate falsehood from the one they love. They hate it when you lie to them, when you are insincere. She would still love you again, even where you did something bad, as bad and sinful as adultery, as long as you were the one who told her how it happened and not another person.

You don't have to lie that you have what you don't have you don't have to lie that her food is sweet when it's not, you don't have to make her feel that you are rich, strong when you are not. The fact is she most likely knows the truth but wants to hear it from you. Don't tell her you are sick, tell her your erection is weak, don't state a quarrel just to avoid having sex with her because you are weak, tell her you don't have a job rather than borrowing from friends to pretend, you cannot do it successfully for long, eventually she would know and that would be a great obstacle to her loving you she might   be   unbearable   for you.

Falsehood can make couple to be bilingual; you would not be able to understand each other. You will be like people from different planet.

Please, please, let the cat out of the bag, tell her the truth and face the consequences, then you begin to live. Falsehood makes you a prisoner of yourself- set yourself free, grow up and give her the chance to love you the way you are. And if she does not am sure someone else will somewhere. First, give her the privilege of knowing who you are, then she might mostly likely love you totally and genuinely.

SELFISHNESS;

There are people that do not have the capacity to love another apart from themselves everything is all about them they will have to be the center of everything or else it will not work. They don't think about another person, no, not even their partner. Actually they don't care, as long as it favor's them. They will have to always comes first.

- They would put on designers but their wife will wear used cloths

- They would always think of their comfort and not that of their wife

- They find fulfillment in their profession or work and would not lift a finger to help their spouse

- Everything begins and must end with them at the center of it all

- They are too blinded by self that they do not know when their spouse need help and attention

- Their own siblings and parents are more special than their spouse, as far as they are concern, nobody else exist

- They would hurt their spouse and have no remorse find it difficult to truly apologizing "am sorry" is not in their vocabulary.

- They are always right, and when they are not, they always have a good excuse

Selfish people are short sighted they never see the big picture that in life you have to be learning constantly and grow to maturity.

Every relationship regardless from both or all the parties involved if life is all about you, you cannot relate effectively. Your partner will feel cheated and bitter, especially where the person is the very opposite of selfishness.

Selfishness many times comes as a result of our upbringing if you are raised in a home that is not a home but a market place where everybody comes to collect something and go where everybody only thinks of self and not any person else. Selfishness can also be as a result of having selfish parents, but what I tell people is that, you might restrain yourself and stop blaming events and people for your actions. If your spouse believes you are selfish, you must try to have a sincere evaluation of yourself.

At least admit the fact that you cannot see yourself like others will, but if people outside your home see you as a caring person, then the next question to ask yourself is that, have you been more kind to people outside than those within your homes or could it be that the people that home are expecting too much from you?

However, there might be the tendency that your spouse just wants more than you are presently giving to them. No worried, give more if you have it to give life is all about receiving. You must see giving to your spouse as a duty and priority; you are obligated to give to them regardless of how you feel towards them or how much they appreciate it. God who sees all will definitely reward you.

We must see our relationship as a seed we sow to life on earth, remember that there is no marriage in heaven. It's a one chance thing; you get to have that opportunity again after life on earth.

Where your spouse is unreasonably greedy, you may have to invite a third party to judge the matter that is of course after you have proofed beyond doubt that you are responsible. try getting someone from her side of the family, when that does not work, you must get an independent body like a counselor to intervene and help educate your spouse and you.It might be easier for her to accept the advice from an independent person rather than yourself.

CHAPTER FIVE

BACK TO HER MAKER

"And he said who told thee that thou wast naked? hast Thou eaten of the tree, where of I commanded thee that thou shouldest not eat?

And the man said, the woman whom thou gavest to be with me, she gave me of the tree and I did eat.

And the lord God said unto the woman what is this that thou hast done? And the woman said, the serpent beguiled me and I did eat.

And the lord God said unto the serpent because thou hast done this, thou are cursed above all cattle, and above every beast of the field; upon thy belly shalt thou go and dust shalt thou eat all the days of thy life.

And I will put enmity between thee and the woman and between thy seed and her seed; it shall bruise thy seed and thou shalt bruise his heel.

Unto the woman he said I will greatly multiply thy sorrow and thy conception, in sorrow thou shalt bring forth children; and thy desire shall unto thy husband and he shall rule over thee.

And unto Adam he said, because thou hast hearkened unto the voice of thy wife, and hast eaten of the tree, of which I commanded thee, saying, thou shalt not eat of it. Cursed is the ground for thy sake; in sorrow shall thou eat of it all the days of thy life;

Thorns also and thistles shall it bring forth to thee; and thou shalt eat the herb of the field.

In the sweat of the face shalt thou eat bread, till thou return unto the ground; for out of it wast thou taken for dust thou art, and unto dust shalt thou return. And Adam called his wife's name Eve; because she was

the mother of all living". Genesis 3:11-20 (King James Version)

In dealing with a woman, it comes a time that you really do not know what to do and sometimes even the woman do not know what to do and sometimes even the woman do not know what is actually wrong and the core reasons behind her reactions or actions. You will have to look at her though the eyes of God's word; first of all, God's word says deals with her with understanding

"Husbands, likewise, dwell with them with understanding, giving honor to the wife, as to the weaker vessel, and as being heirs together of the grace of life, that your prayers may be hindered". 1Peter 3:7, New King James

Talk to God, tell him about your wife, I mean telling him your dissatisfactions and challenges. As you do that you will have to open up your spirit to receive instructions from him. You may not even have a clue on what to do but once you sincerely lord back to God for answers, you will find the answers you seek. That is where humility comes to play you might be missing it and don't know it, Kenneth Hagin said "you may think you have faith but you don't" so I say "you may think you have understanding but you don't". only God in certain situation can help you out. If you have messed up, the first step is always to go back to your creator and hers, ask him for forgiveness and pled for mercy. Admit you are wrong and give time for her to receive your apology even though God has forgiven you. God forgives immediately you ask genuinely but she is not God because she does not see your heart, God does.

Its God at this point that will tell you what to do, remember, he created her. He knows the key to unlock that door of her heart. Some people just start buying gifts and all the woman actually wants is for him to spend time with her. It could be anything; maybe your sexual life together, your relationship with her siblings, parents, friends etc.

you may get for started trying to search for solution.

Spend time with God, talking not complaining but literally pouring out your heart to God. The truth is that as he (God) sees your genuineness, he at the same time relates to her, especially if she has a relationship with God. Believe me she will come around.

Remember that God can reach her through other people not just you. It becomes difficult if everybody around her looks up to her for advice. But, God knows how to create an experience that she can relate with. One woman was so angry with her husband that she left the house, she got to her parent's place and was met with the same temptation that her husband fell into, she didn't fall but somehow she saw why he fell and immediately parked her things and went back home. He was praying for her, he didn't give upon the relationship, he trusted God to resort his home and God did. Always remember that God is the initiator of marriage and can resort every marriage if he is invited and allowed to handle it. The creator knows the right mixture to get desired taste.

The good thing about going back to her creator is that you are with that act trusting in his ability to intervene and the beauty of it is that he works both ways. He also has ministering spirits that could reach both of you at the same time regardless their location. Having your marriage in the right place requires faith; you cannot receive anything from God if you don't have faith in him to that thing.

Some people have developed them to receive healing, success in business, ministry etc. but have not taken time out to actually develop their faith in the area of marriage. They easily give up when it comes to their wife.

Remember that faith connect you to the realm of all possibilities.

Now in God back to her creator; you will also have to see his manuscript on what is required of your husband, father and brother to her because that's who you are.

Life on earth is not so long, even if you live for two hundred years (200 years), it's still short. I remember when I was in my thirties and saw those in their fifties as old, but when I turned fifty I realized that life is short; it was just like yesterday. It's so short we don't have to waste it holding on to foolish pride. You have eternity to live after death. If God would refuse to answer your prayers because of your relationship with your wife, then it must be very important to him. I cannot imagine my son calling me and I will not answer him, I must be very angry and I have not gotten to that level of anger, how much more a loving father like God.

"The Lord has appeared of old to me, saying:" yes, I have loved you with an everlasting love, therefore with loving kindness I have drawn you". Jeremiah 31:3, New King James.

"For I am persuaded that neither death nor life, nor angels nor principalities nor power, nor things present nor things to come, nor height nor depth, nor any other created thing, shall be able to separate us from the love of God when is in Christ Jesus our Lord". Romans 8:38, New King James

As you go before God, you might just see where you or her is missing it; it may be that all you needed to have done was to help to pursue her own goal in life, help her to find her place of fulfillment and purpose. Help her find what she loves and enjoy doing. You also may just be patient with her, wait on her to discover herself. When people have not discovered themselves they become a burden on those around them. You may have to help her to also believe in herself. God, am sure will open your eyes to what you need to do.

In raping this book up I must say that, I know she must have annoyed or upset you but you must look beyond the hurt and see her heart and intentions.

"*Love covers a multitude of sin*".

You must try to look away from some of her actions and let God give you directions on what to do. It may take time and am not promising that it will be short but time has a way of healing wounds in the heart.

I generally do not encourage separation unless there is a threat of life; physically or emotionally. Some people won't kill you but they can make you mad, I mean literally go insane you may need some space to be able to be sure you can handle the situation. Some hearts are so wounded that it will take a miracle for them to be healed, miracles are what they are, miracles. Some people are also messed up that they shouldn't be married in the first place, it's near impossible to live with such people. God can still help, but if you are sure you can handle it, please be sincere with yourself and to God then with your spouse.

Some session of counseling may help, therapy sessions also and sometimes spiritual deliverance sessions. If you personally don't give up faith, then there is hope but when you cannot take it, please start by having a break, from the relationship and put what happen next into the hands of God, being sincere to yourself and God. In many ways we give up because we actually want better and not willing to make better. Holding on so tightly to the hurt experienced in the past. Let me simply say that wounds take time to heal and we must be willing to give that time for healing to take place, time depending on the personalities involved.

Email me anointedabundance2005@gmail.com or call ±2348066241512

www.ingramcontent.com/pod-product-compliance
Lightning Source LLC
Chambersburg PA
CBHW061444160726
47995CB00003B/1037